Resume Help For Success

Simple Resume Writing Tips, Resume Examples & Sample Cover Letters

By
Faith M. Davis

Income Disclaimer

This book contains business strategies, marketing methods and other business advice that, regardless of my own results and experience, may not produce the same results (or any results) for you. I make absolutely no guarantee, expressed or implied, that by following the advice below you will make any money or improve current profits, as there are several factors and variables that come into play regarding any given business.
Primarily, results will depend on the nature of the product or business model, the conditions of the marketplace, the experience of the individual, and situations and elements that are beyond your control.

As with any business endeavor, you assume all risk related to investment and money based on your own discretion and at your own potential expense.

Liability Disclaimer

By reading this book, you assume all risks associated with using the advice given below, with a full understanding that you, solely, are responsible for anything that may occur as a result of putting this information into action in any way, and regardless of your interpretation of the advice.

You further agree that our company cannot be held responsible in any way for the success or failure of your business as a result of the information presented in this book. It is your responsibility to conduct your own due diligence regarding the safe and successful operation of your business if you intend to apply any of our information in any way to your business operations.

Terms of Use

You are given a non-transferable, "personal use" license to this book. You cannot distribute it or share it with other individuals.

Also, there are no resale rights or private label rights granted when purchasing this book. In other words, it's for your own personal use only.

Resume Help For Success

Simple Resume Writing Tips, Resume Examples & Sample Cover Letters

Table of Contents

Introduction

Having a strong resume can mean the difference between landing the job and not landing the job. To succeed, you will need a resume that is professionally written and that reflects you, your job abilities, and your experience in a way that sets you apart from the pack.

A resume is the first impression you will make on your potential employers, and we all know how important first impressions are. For that reason, it should be your number one priority. But I guess you already knew that or you wouldn't have purchased this book!

There are many ways you can go about crafting a resume that works, but there is no magic formula for a resume that will work in every situation. Every resume should have some uniquenesses that make it stand out, and that is why there isn't one simple template for everyone, but there are specific elements you will need to include in your resume that every employer looks for.

It is not difficult to put together a resume that works, especially since you have this book to guide you, but it is important that you not overlook what makes your resume most effective. This one-page resume, along with your cover letter, is all you have to present yourself, your abilities, your experience, your education, and your accomplishments. It is what will compel the business owner or manager to pick up the phone and call you for an interview.

If you've done any research online, you have probably discovered that there are many schools of thought regarding how a resume should look, what information it should contain, and how to put it together. There are some fundamentals, however, that most business people agree about, such as that a resume should be concise, to the point, and easy to read.

No matter what school of thought you subscribe to, it is imperative that your resume is what potential employers want to see. You'll want as much information about resumes as possible so you can create one that represents you well and that you will be proud to send out as an introduction of you and what you can do for a company.

What you will find inside the pages of this book is a comprehensive guide that will provide you with everything you need to know about resume writing. I will present you with a few different ways of crafting a resume so you can choose the one that best suits your personality and your objectives. We will cover the important components of the resume and cover letter, along with ways to make yours stand out. I have included numerous tips and tricks you can use to make sure your resume gets noticed over other applicants.

While we're at it, I'll also provide you with some advice about job interviewing and what you can do to land the job at that stage. Simply filling out a job application and waiting for a call won't manifest the job of your dreams. It takes persistence and skill on your part, as well as having the right tools at your disposal. I'll give you the tools, so you can gain the skills you need. Match that with your own persistence and a positive mindset and you're sure to get the job you seek in no time!

Resume Writing at a Glance

A resume is an important sales tool that outlines your skills and experiences, so an employer can see at a glance how you can contribute to their company. Your resume has to sell you in short order.

How to Gain Interest in 15 Seconds

While you may have all the requirements for a particular position, if your resume does not portray that clearly and the employer does not instantly come to the conclusion that you "have what it takes," your resume is not doing the job it should. Believe it or not, an employer will usually not give your resume more than a 15-second glance to determine whether it will move on to the "consider file" or the "reject file." That's nothing to mess around with, so you'll want to be sure you grab their attention immediately.

Some people think of a resume as their "life on a page," but how could anyone put everything important about himself or herself on a single piece of paper? Resumes are actually meant to be much more specific, including only the most relevant information about you for a specific job.

The most effective resumes are focused on a specific job title and address the employer's stated requirements for the position. Although it takes a little more work on your part, the more information you gain beforehand about the duties and skills required for the job, the better shot you have of getting past the 15 second mark and making the "consider" list. This is because employers appreciate when an applicant goes the extra mile before they are even hired. It demonstrates to them the kind of work they can expect out of you moving forward, and proves to them that you care more about the position than others who sent out general resumes. By customizing your resume, you immediately move up a few notches in the employer's eyes, therefore it is one of the most important steps you can take.

Instead of just providing information about jobs you've held in the past and skills you have that MIGHT relate to the job at hand, you will be providing the accomplishments, skills and experience you have that is most relevant for each individual position you apply to; therefore, you will want to capture as much information about the employer and the position as you can so you can tailor your resume to fit each specific job.

You will want to create a master resume copy that depicts everything you bring to the table, and then from that master copy, you can customize each version according to the specific job you are applying to. In this way, you will create the least amount of work for yourself because you will just need to tweak a couple parts of the resume each time you apply for a job.

The Evolution of the Resume

Just like life, a resume is always growing and changing. As your career goals shift or the job market changes, and as you grow personally and professionally, chances are you will need to rewrite your resume or at least create new versions of it. Writing a resume is a lifelong process.

The best way to keep on top of this is to update your resume to a new version each time you add a skill or acquire new experience. In doing that, it will be easy to get a job quickly should the need arise in the future. You'll be able to just pull up your resume, customize it to the position you are applying to and send it out, without having to spend a lot of time revising it.

Deciding What Goes on Your Resume

How do you know what parts of your life (past, present, and future) are most important to prospective employers? How do you select which information to include? The quick answer to these questions is that it depends. I know that's not what you want to hear because it would be much easier to be given a simple outline to follow, but it really does depend on your individual career goals, as well as on the professional goals of the companies you are applying to.

In the end, only you, through research, planning, questioning and self-reflection, can determine the shape and content of your resume. The good news, however, is that the strategies included in this book can help you ask the right questions so you can begin exploring your options.

The Truth About Resumes And the Job Search

Depending on whom you ask, a resume may be viewed as the single most important vehicle to securing your next job, or it may be viewed as an unnecessary nuisance. Both are actually incorrect.

A resume is a professional introduction meant to encourage the opportunity for communication through an in-person interview, which has the potential to lead to a job offer.

Rarely is a person hired by his or her resume alone, and it is just as rare to be offered an interview without one.

A resume is usually the first line of contact. It establishes the first impression of a potential job candidate's skills, background and hiring value. If written well, this impression can be a positive one, offering the reader a sense of the candidate's "fit" for the position and company being targeted.

If written really well, it may convince the reader that the job candidate is ideally suited for the job. When coupled with an effective cover letter, the resume can be a strong marketing tool, selling an employer on the fact that you are the one for the job.

Preparing a resume may be time-consuming, but having a well-constructed, well-designed resume is an important part of your job search. You must remember that for each available job opening, there may be as many as 100 to 1000 resumes submitted. If your resume fails to adequately and accurately convey your hiring value (for the specific position), fails to establish your hiring value over competing candidates, or is difficult to follow, your ability to compete against those 100 to 1000 professionals vying for the same position will be greatly diminished.

If your resume secures an interview, it has done its job. If it sets you ahead of the competition in the mind of your interviewer, then it has given you a distinct advantage, and has gone beyond its job.

A great resume does what all good marketing pieces do: it sells the "consumer" (the potential employer or hiring manager) on the "product" (you).

Like it or not, the task of looking for employment is actually like having a temporary job in sales and marketing. The product you are "selling" is you, and the "customer" needs to be sold on the fact that you have what it takes to get the job done and to meet the needs of the position based on his or her unique needs.

The employer is going to want to know how you are going to solve his or her problems, and he or she is going to give your resume about 15 seconds or less to sell this. 15 seconds is the average time a hiring manager will allot to a new resume before giving it a potential "yes" or "no" response.

The resume alone will not usually get you the job, but it can certainly secure your chances of being seen and interviewed, just as it can cause you to be passed over in favor of a candidate who offers a better presentation.

As with any type of marketing campaign, use your resume as one tool in your search. Continue to network, improve your interviewing skills, and use every avenue available to better your chances and opportunities.

Essentially, a resume is YOU in short form on paper. That is why having a compelling, good looking, easy-to-read resume is so important. In the next chapter, we'll look at what makes up a winning resume, so yours can be all that it needs to be.

The Elements of a Winning Resume

Although many resume templates have been created to make your job application chances improve, you should aim to create a resume that is different from the pack. Templates should be viewed as a guide, and you should add your own spin so you stand out. Still, it is important that your resume follow certain guidelines:

Construction:

A professional resume must be well written. It should not have any grammatical, spelling or construction errors. Since your resume is your first point of contact with a potential employer, you surely don't want to commit any mistakes that can be easily avoided. Any employer would be turned off by mistakes like these, because it shows them that you are not thorough or neat in your work. A resume can be viewed as a sample of the work you would do for that employer; therefore you should treat it as such.

Image:

Professional resumes should be attractive and different. Unique people attract immediate attention, and so do resumes. Make sure you create a unique and attention-grabbing resume in order to improve your chances of getting noticed. Just be sure you are attracting good attention!

Accuracy:

A professional resume should be accurate. It should contain true facts about you. It should reflect you as a person and as a professional. It should state your experiences, education, and your achievements. Enumerate them in such a way that the reader would be impressed, but be sure to be accurate and real.

Potential:

A professional resume should show your potential and demonstrate how you can contribute to the organization in a way that others can't. Instead of bragging about you, a well-crafted resume will outline an applicant's strengths in a way that is favorable to the employer. At the same time, be confident in your abilities. If an employer wants to hire you, it's because they have a need to fulfill. You obviously have a need to fulfill as well (getting a job), but you don't want to come off as needy or having low self esteem.

Clarity in Short:

A short and concise resume speaks volumes. Your resume is not a novel. It is meant to highlight the important points that would make you qualified for the position. Show that you value the employer's time by keeping it short and clear.

Cover Letter:

A professional resume should be introduced by a well-written cover letter. Just as peanut butter and jelly go together, so do the resume and cover letter. The cover letter adds a dimension to your resume that cannot be reached without it. You will learn more about how to write your best cover letter later in this book.

Preparation Keys

Before you write, take time to do a self-assessment on paper. Outline your skills and abilities, as well as your work experience and extracurricular activities. This will make it easier to prepare a thorough resume.

When you do this, be sure to write down dates as well because they can be very important in the eye of the employer – especially in showing that you have a consistent work history. Gaps in work history do not bear well with potential employers as it gives the impression that you are not reliable.

Gather together the names of the businesses you have worked for along with their address and phone number and the name of your immediate supervisor at the time. Do not include salary history on a general resume. If salary comes up, it will be during the interview or at the time you are offered the job.

Note special achievements and awards you have received along with the date you received them. You may also want to include a blurb about the qualifications that needed to be met in order to receive that award.

In preparing your resume, the more you know about the job position and the company, the better. The key things you want to know are: the company's missions and goals, the needs of the position, the company's concerns, and who makes up the company's competition. I'll tell you right now that these are not things that most people look into before applying for a job, and it will make you much more prepared so that you can stand out above the rest.

What goes along with that is assessing yourself and your unique skills and experience to be able to depict how you can fulfill the needs of the employer best.

With this information ready to go, you will have the material necessary to create an effective marketing piece (your resume).

Preparing the Summary Section

As in any type of marketing material, it is important to present the information so that it captures your customer's interest quickly. Your goal is to encourage the reader to stay with your document as long as possible. Your chance for a more detailed reading increases when you give the reader the information that he or she is seeking early in the resume.

One of the best ways to accomplish this is to create a Summary Section at the beginning of your resume. A Summary Section highlights the personal and professional skills you possess that allow you to excel in your chosen field and position.

Items and skills of greatest importance (from your readers' viewpoint) should be listed in priority, supporting an impression of both "fit" and potential success. In addition, these should be aspects of your background that set you apart from your competing candidates, particularly candidates with skill sets similar to your own.

In short, the summary demonstrates to your reader how you will solve their problems better than others and it explains why interviewing you would be a worthwhile use of their valuable time.

Always Remember It's Not About You

Although you might argue that your resume is about you, it actually isn't. While it outlines the skills and experience you have for a given job position, it does so to conclude that the company's needs will be met. It's really all about them. If you can keep that first and foremost in your mind as you craft your resume, you will create a winner!

Think about it from the perspective of the employer. Step into their shoes and imagine you need to fill a position at your company. Imagine how badly you need someone that you can trust and that will make your investment of time and money pay off. Keep imagining yourself as that person as you read the resumes that come in. What would you be looking for?

You would want someone who 1) understands your company and your needs, and 2) can be the answer to your prayers. You aren't looking for someone tooting his or her own horn, because you really don't care. What you care about is what they can do for you.

The interview is your opportunity for negotiation where you get to discuss what you get out of the deal. But at the resume stage, the only person that matters is your reader. They hold all the marbles.

Write your resume so that they can see that you are the answer to their prayers and so that they feel that you will fill a void for them. Then, you will have a wining resume!

Preparing the Benefits You Offer

It is expensive to hire someone, train them, and then let someone go. The employer wants to make sure that does not happen. All parties involved want to know they are making the right decision, and it is your job to assure them that they are.

The most effective way to do this is by identifying how you have benefited employers in the past.

Take credit for your participation and accomplishments. While looking at the aspects of your background may seem minor or of little value to you, they may be seen as valuable assets to those looking to fill a need, so don't downplay anything.

Arranging Your Layout

The layout of your resume is extremely important. Your resume needs to maintain a "clean" and professional appearance. Remember, it is representing you!

Your resume should allow the reader to access the information they seek quickly and easily. Neat margins, adequate "white space" between groupings and the use of indenting all aid in legibility and retention of the material.

While the use of bolded and italicized text can often be effective, be sure that you don't go overboard. Overuse of these features actually diminishes the effectiveness of promoting the material they are intended to highlight.

Multi-Page Resumes

The standards for resume length have changed over the years. It used to be typical for resumes to be one-page in length, and no longer. For candidates with years of experience having held multiple positions or with outstanding achievements, this one-page constraint often results in a document that is unreadable, looks "squashed," or utilizes a font size so small that the reader is required to squint (which they won't actually bother to do). Because of this, the one-page standard no longer holds true.

Use as much space as you need to concisely, accurately, and effectively communicate your skills, history, achievements, and accomplishments as they relate to the position and company being targeted.

A two-page document, if presented well, will not diminish the effectiveness of your marketing strategy - as long as the information you provide is relevant and valuable to your reader's goals and interests, and as long as you have kept that information concise and easy to read.

A three-page resume is requiring much of your reader's time (and patience), and may not be as effective as a more concise presentation. In academic fields and European markets, it may be necessary to go over two pages in length, but only provide this much information if you absolutely cannot present your history and achievements in less space.

If you are including additional pages, be certain that your name is on the secondary pages. Consider including your phone number on those pages as well in case they become separated.

How do you put together a resume that will get attention? Let's now take a look at each section one by one.

Resume Components

While all resumes will differ (and they should so that you stand out), there are certain components that a resume should always contain, such as: the heading, the objective, your experience, your education, skills and qualifications, and awards and achievements. Let's look at these components in detail now:

The Heading

The heading of your resume provides basic contact information about you, including: your name, address telephone number and your email address.

Your contact information is essentially the most important information in the entire document because if they can't contact you, the resume is pointless. Make certain your name, address, phone number, and e-mail address are clearly visible and at the top of your document (from habit, that is where your reader will look for this information - do not make them search for it).

You can arrange this information in a variety of ways. The simplest way is like this:

John Doe

123 Resume Lane

Hiremeville, PA 19040

Home Phone: (555) 555-5555

Cell Phone: (555) 444-4444

email: johndoe@gotthatjob.com

As you can see, the name is in larger print than the rest of the information and it is bolded. The rest of the contact information is in smaller print and is not bolded.

Another format you can use for the heading looks like this:

John Doe

123 Resume Lane • Hiremeville, PA 19040

Home: (555) 555-5555 • Cell: (555) 444-4444

johndoe@gotthatjob.com

Yet another way that you can construct the heading is as follows:

John Doe

123 Resume Lane

Hiremeville, PA 19040

Home: (555) 555-5555 • Cell: (555) 444-4444

johndoe@gotthatjob.com

The important thing to remember about the heading is that it contains your up-to-date pertinent contact information and highlights your name. Here are some other pointers to remember when writing the heading of your resume:

- Avoid nicknames.

- Use a permanent address. If you are a student in transit, use your parents' address, a friend's address, or the address you plan to use after graduation.

- Use a permanent telephone number and include the area code. NOTE: Be sure to record a neutral, friendly greeting on your voicemail before you send out your resumes.

- Add your email address. Many employers will find it useful. NOTE: Choose an email address that sounds professional.

- Include your website address only if the webpage reflects your professional ambitions.

The Objective Statement

An objective tells potential employers the sort of work you're hoping to do. There are two schools of thought regarding an objective statement. Some people say you shouldn't include this on a resume because that is what your cover letter is for. Other people say that stating what you want to accomplish in your career is probably the most important part of the resume. In my opinion, it is important to include an objective statement because you cannot guarantee that the cover letter will always stay with the resume. If they get separated, the objective statement will serve an important part of your resume.

The objective must state clearly what you are applying for. In short, positive and upbeat language (avoid exaggerations), state the position you desire and the skill and the experience that makes you qualified for it. The objective is your opening line and like many advertisements, it should be meaningful and packed with quality words that will hold your readers attention without sounding superfluous. If that fails, you can bet that your resume takes a highway to the trash bin and the employer moves onto another one.

There are some important tips you will want to know. First and foremost, this statement should be brief and concise, no more than a sentence or two.

Be specific about the job you want. An example might be, "To obtain an entry-level position within a financial institution requiring strong analytical and organizational skills." Tailor your objective to each employer you target and each job you seek.

Objective statements improve your resume by helping you:

- Emphasize your main qualifications and summarize them for the employer.

- Inform the employer of the position(s) you are seeking and your career goals.

- Establish your professional identity.

As discussed earlier, to improve your chances for success, it is always a good idea to tailor your objective statement (as well as your whole resume and cover letter) to particular organizations and/or positions. This means, for example, calling a position by the name the company uses to describe it. You might even indicate the organization's name in your statement.

Strive to match your qualifications with those desired by the organization. If you are unsure what the employers will be looking for, you'll need to do some research to give your objective statement a competitive edge.

I have now included some questions that will help you draft your objective statement. By answering as many of the following questions as possible, you'll have the information in front of you that you need to write an outstanding objective statement.

About you:

- What are your main qualifications (strengths, skills, areas of expertise)?

- What positions (or range of positions) do you seek?

- What are your professional goals?

- What type of organizations or work settings are you interested in working at?

About the Company or Organization:

- Which of your qualifications are most desired by the employer?

- What position titles (or range or positions) are available?

- What are some goals of the organizations that interest you?

- What types of organizations or work settings are now hiring?

Common Objective Writing Mistakes:

What is wrong with the following objective statement?

> "To have the opportunity to work hard, prove my skills, and be challenged so that my training and education would be utilized."

Does it contain the right purpose of a resume objective statement? Is it attractive enough to make the reader consider this person for an interview?

All the answers would be a big "NO!" So what's wrong with this statement?

There are too many self-serving words. No matter how bad you want a job, if your resume objective contains self-serving words, you will never have any chance of getting an interview.

Employers seek applicants who can help improve the present state of their business. Remember also that the employer is not and will never be interested to what you want.

A resume objective should state what you could do for the company, and not the other way around. You can be very specific by stating your contributions to your previous employers. Doing this would give you a good chance in making it to the interview. Say you were able to increase the previous company's sales by 40%. Don't be too shy or modest to mention that. Wouldn't the reader be very interested in meeting you face to face if he thinks you could do the same for his company?

The most common mistake made in writing objective statements is being too general and vague in describing either the position desired or your qualifications. For example, some objective statements read like this:

"An internship allowing me to utilize my knowledge and expertise in different areas."

Such an objective statement raises more questions than it answers: What kind of internship? What knowledge? What kinds of expertise? Which areas? Be as specific as possible in your objective statement to help your readers see what you have to offer at a glance.

To help you come up with an objective statement that is effective, I have included several formulas for you, starting on the next page.

Formula 1: Emphasize a Particular Position & Your Relevant Qualifications:

Option 1: A position as a [name or type of position] allowing me to use my [qualifications].

Example: A position as a Support Specialist allowing me to use my skills in the fields of computer science and management information systems.

Option 2: To utilize my [qualifications] as a [position title].

Example: To utilize my computer science and management information systems skills as a Support Specialist.

Formula 2:   To Emphasize the Field or Type of Organization You Want to Work in & Your Professional Goal or Your Main Qualifications:

Option 1: An opportunity to [professional goal] in a [type of organization, work environment, or field].

Example: An opportunity to obtain a loan officer position, with eventual advancement to vice president for lending services, in a growth-oriented bank.

Option 2: To enter [type of organization, work environment, or field] allowing me to use my [qualifications].

Example: To join an aircraft research team allowing me to apply my knowledge of avionics and aircraft electrical systems.

Formula 3: To Emphasize Your Professional or Career Goal or an Organizational Goal:

Option 1: To [professional goal].

Example: To help children and families in troubled situations by utilizing my child protection services background.

Option 2: An opportunity to [professional goal].

Example: An opportunity to help children and families in troubled situations by utilizing my child protection services background.

Formula 4: To Explain a Specific Position Desired & Your Specialization:

Option 1: [Position name] specializing in [what you specialize in].

Example: Technical writer specializing in user documentation.

Some things to keep in mind when formulating your objective statement include the following:

- Integrate key words and phrases used in the job advertisement(s).

- Play with word choices to fit your strengths and the employer's expectations. You might try some of the following, for example:

  Substitute the word "use" with words like: "develop," "apply," or "employ."

Replace the phrase "allowing me" with words like: "requiring" or "giving me the opportunity."

Change the word "enter" to words like: "join," "pursue," "obtain," "become a member" or "contribute."

- Blend two or more of the above generic models or create your own!

Depending on the format of your resume, the objective section should be written in sentence format with its own heading, and it should be at the top of your resume under your contact information.

The Body of Your Resume

The body of the resume starts after the objective and includes everything else on the resume. It should revolve around strengthening your objective. Remember that the employer is looking for specific qualifications and experience that should match the job at hand.

The body of your resume should be bulleted as much as possible to allow for easy reading and scanning, and at the very least, it should match the requirements the company is looking for.

Design your key phrases to stand out. Better yet, place yourself in the interviewer's shoes; give him all the necessary information that can possibly be absorbed in a quick glance at your resume. Reserve the details for the interview. The important thing now is to hold the potential employer's attention.

Remember to include action words throughout the body of your resume. You can get a good idea as to the action words that would stand out to the employer by reading the advertisement they posted to find job applicants.

NOTE: The next two sections of the resume are interchangeable depending on which applies the most to the position you are applying for. If you think your job experience is more relevant to the job, then list "job experience" next. If it is your education that will help most, then put that section next. If you are a student, your education will most likely come first unless you have had some relevant internships.

Job Experience

This is the most complex section of your resume, and it is required, although you have a great deal of freedom in the way you present your experiences.

To get started on this section, make a list of your job titles and the names, dates and locations of places where you worked. Document your most recent 10-15 years of employment and/or experience – longer if the most recent position extended 10 years or more. Be certain to document growth in a company where multiple positions have been held, including identification of promotions and increased responsibilities.

Break each job (paid or unpaid) into short, descriptive phrases or sentences that begin with action verbs. These phrases will highlight the skills you used on the job, and help the employer envision you as an active person in the workplace. Use action words to describe the work you did.

You may choose special typestyles, **bolded text**, <u>underlined text</u>, *italicized text,* or specific placement to draw your reader's attention to the information you want to emphasize. For example, when the company you worked for is more impressive than your job title, you may want to highlight that information.

List positions held prior to this in decreasing detail, unless a previous position more effectively documents relevant skills for the position you are currently targeting.

You want to entice the employer into wanting to meet you to learn more (the interview). Current history and recently utilized skills will hold the most value.

Remember, you will have an opportunity to expand on the information in your resume during the interview. So, entice your reader to want to learn more, but don't forget to leave something to tell.

Briefly give the employer an overview of work that has taught you specific skills. Include your work experience in reverse chronological order (last job first, working backward to your first, relevant job last).

Here is a list of what should be included:

- Title of position

- Name of organization

- Location of work (town, state)

- Dates of employment

- Describe your work responsibilities with emphasis on specific skills and achievements.

You probably should not go back more than your three previous jobs so that your resume doesn't get too long. However, you will want to include any job experience that is relevant to the job you are applying for to show you have experience in that field, so if you think it will help you, going beyond three may be wise in some cases.

Depending on how you are formatting your resume, there are a couple of ways that you can put this section together. Here are some examples:

Option 1:

April, 1998 -   XYZ Corporation; Anywhere, IL
Present   Sales Analyst

Duties: To monitor sales activities for 20 sales people, calculate profit/loss margins, make suggestions for improvement, hold educational seminars to insure sales are progressing as they should, prepare annual statements, formulate and implement new procedures to improve efficiency.

Option 2:

XYZ Corporation; Anywhere, IL
April, 1998 – Present
Position: Sales Analyst

Duties: To monitor sales activities for 20 sales people, calculate, profit/loss margins, make suggestions for improvement, hold educational seminars to insure sales is progressing as it should, prepare annual statements, formulate and implement new procedures to improve efficiency

Option 3:

XYZ Corporation; Anywhere, IL

April, 1998 – Present

Sales Analyst

- Monitor sales activities for 20 sales people
- Calculate, profit/loss margins
- Make suggestions for improvement
- Hold educational seminars to insure sales is progressing as it should
- Prepare annual statements
- Formulate and implement new procedures to improve efficiency

There are many more ways that you can layout this section and it all depend on how your whole resume is laid out. As long as you have the basic information about what company you worked for, when you worked for them, your position at the company, and your job duties, and as long as it is easily read, then you should be covered.

Education

This section can be set up much like the job experience section and it all really depends on what format you are choosing for your resume. This section is an important one for most students, and it is a required element of the resume. In this section, you should include:

- The name and location of your college or university (Your most recent educational information is listed first).

- Your degree (A.S., B.S., B.A., etc.) and graduation date.

- Your major(s) and your minor(s) concentration.

- Add your grade point average (GPA) if it is higher than 3.0.

- Mention any academic honors you may have received.

Use placement of information, **bolded type**, <u>underlined type</u> or *italicized type* to highlight the features you want to emphasize. It is sometimes necessary to pinpoint a feature or features that make you stand out among other students.

For example, students bold their university or college if they feel like that is a distinctive feature. Others may decide to bold their type of degree.

Here are two examples of education sections, with different information emphasized:

Option 1:

Purdue University, West Lafayette, Indiana
Bachelor of Science, May 1999
Major: Supervision: GPA 5.5/6.0

Option 2:

Bachelor of Science in Accounting, May 1999
Minor in Finance, GPA: 5.5/6.0 Major, 5.2/6.0 Overall
Purdue University, West Lafayette, Indiana

In your education section, you may want to include a couple of sub-groups, especially if you are a recent graduate looking for your first position. One such sub-group could be: "Related Course Work."

This is an optional part of your Education section, which can be quite impressive and informative for potential employers. Students seeking internships may want to list all completed major-related courses.

Graduates might list job-related courses differently than those required to receive the degree (employers will already be aware of those). Include high-level courses in optional concentrations, foreign languages, computer applications or communications classes, for example. You may choose more meaningful headings such as "Computer Applications" if you wish to emphasize particular areas.

Remember, employers and recruiters are familiar with the basic courses required in your major; therefore limit these sections to special courses or skills you have to offer.

Another optional sub-group in the education section is "Special Projects." This optional section may be added to point out special features of your education that are particularly interesting to employers or that may make you more qualified than others for the job you are seeking.

Students often include research, writing, or computer projects. Limit your description to the most important facts related to the position you seek. You may expand your discussion in your application letter.

If you like, you can include any awards you received or special achievements in this section, but most resumes will have a separate section for this to cover not only academic awards but also business awards.

Skills and Qualifications

While not all resumes contain a skills section, this may be helpful when you want to emphasize the skills you have acquired from your various jobs or activities, rather than the duties, or the job title.

If you do not have enough previous experience for the specific job you are seeking for, it is important to emphasize your skills pertaining to that job. Skills can be just as important as work experience to employers.

To prepare this section you should:

- List jobs, activities, projects and special offices.

- Think of skills you have gained through those experiences.

- Group these skills into 3-5 job related skills categories and use them as headings.

- List your skills with significant details under the headings.

- Arrange headings in order of importance as they relate to your career objective.

- Arrange skills under headings in order of importance according to your goal.

In this section, you will also want to include any office machines you have experience operating, software programs you have become proficient in, and anything else that you feel might put you over the top with the job.

Example:

Leadership

- Conducted monthly club and board meetings for Lafayette Junior Woman's Club.
- Headed club's $8,000 philanthropic project sponsored by Tippecanoe County Historical Association.
- Coordinated responsibilities of committees to sell and serve food to 1500 people at fundraiser.

Business Communication

- Completed a formal report for Business Writing course.
- Wrote annual state and district reports of all club's community service projects, volunteered hours and monetary donations.
- Compiled, type, mimeographed and distributed club books to each member.

Financial Management

- Supervised the collection and dispersion of $4,000 in funds to various agencies and projects.

- Wrote and analyzed periodic business statements regarding funds to specific projects/agencies.

Awards and Achievements

The next section of your resume can be worded in a couple of different ways. This is where you want to let the potential employer know you have participated in activities and events, as well as any professional organizations you are a member of and any special awards you have received.

A lot of this depends on whether or not you are fresh out of school looking for your first job or if you have already been in the business world and are applying for another job.

You can choose a few different ways to word this section. It can be titled: "Activities and Honors" or "Awards and Organizations" or any other title that is appropriate. You have to tailor your resume to your specific needs as well as towards what type of job you are applying for.

This optional section points out your leadership, sociability and energy level as shown by your involvement in different activities. This should be your shortest section and should support your career objective. Additional information about activities can be included in your application letter or discussed at your interview.

In this section, be sure to:

- Select only activities and honors that support your career objective.

- List your college or professional organizations and arrange them in order of importance as they relate to your career objective.

- Include any office or official positions you have held.

- Spell out any acronyms your employer may not recognize.

- Include dates.

Example:

Accounting Club, President

Alpha Zeta Professional Fraternity

Purdue Grand Prix Foundation, President

Purdue Association for the Education of Young Children (PAEYC)

For awards, you should always include the year you received the award. You also may want to include a brief explanation of the criteria that you had to meet in order to get that honor.

References

This is the shortest section of your resume, because it should only consist of one sentence: "References are available upon request." You should generally not include references with your resume. You will put your references on a separate reference sheet, which we will address in the next section.

If the job you are applying for asks in the ad to include references when you send in your resume, you should change the "References" section to read: "References are attached." Then include the reference sheet after the resume

Your Reference Sheet

The reference sheet is an important part of your job search process. Employers will often request references and many of them will actually call the individuals you refer them to. You will want to have several different people on hand who will vouch for you as far as your character, your work habits, your work ethics, and your general value and worth as an employee and person.

You will want to have a minimum of three references and no more than five. At least one of these references should be a personal reference that is not a relative. It can be a friend, a co-worker, or an acquaintance. The others should be work or school references.

The first rule of thumb for references is to ask the person first if you can use them as a reference when applying for jobs. As long as you have a good relationship with them, most people are happy to vouch for you and give you a glowing recommendation.

The purpose of a reference sheet is to have a list of people who can verify and elaborate on your professional experience for a potential employer. Past employers, professors, and advisors are the best professional references to have.

It is important to have a reference sheet on hand because potential employers will often ask for a list of references they can contact. If you included a statement such as "References Available upon Request" on your resume, you should be able to produce a reference sheet as soon as one is requested. In any case, having a reference sheet on hand will save you time later during the interview process, and will portray you as a person who is prepared.

Make sure to include people who know what type of person you are and who are familiar with your work. It is important to select individuals who know your distinctiveness so that they can provide a positive and accurate description of you to the employer or company in which you are seeking employment.

You should ALWAYS contact your references before including them on a reference sheet. It is also a good idea to give them a copy of your resume and talk to them about the job you are seeking so they will know how to best represent you.

When you are listing your references, you should include the following information:

- Your name

- Your present and permanent address (es)

- Your reference person(s)' information, including:

  o Name

  o Department/Company

  o Title/Position

  o Address

  o Telephone number

  o Brief statement as to how you know this person. (It is not required to include this part, but it can help. That way if a potential employer does check your references, they know why you wanted to list them on your reference sheet.)

Your Cover Letter

The purpose of a cover letter is to introduce you and your resume, and to provide some additional information to the potential employers about yourself. You may also want to point out certain parts of your resume that you want the employer to pay special attention to.

An individually typed cover letter should accompany each resume you send out. Your cover letter may make the difference between obtaining a job interview and having your resume ignored; therefore it makes sense to devote the necessary time and effort to writing powerful cover letters.

A cover letter should complement, not duplicate your resume. Its purpose is to interpret the data-oriented, factual resume and add a personal touch. A cover letter is often your earliest written contact with a potential employer, creating a critical first impression.

There are three different kinds of cover letters:

1) **_The Application Letter:_** This type of cover letter responds to a specific job opening you have seen advertised.

2) **_The Prospecting Letter:_** This letter inquires about any job openings.

3) **_The Networking Letter:_** This type of cover letter requests information and assistance in your job search.

If you are sending out a resume, your cover letter should always include a line that says where you found the advertisement for the job you are applying for. If you saw it in a newspaper, be sure to underline the name of the newspaper (grammar rules count!)

You should always tailor your cover letter to the specific job you are applying for. While it is certainly easier to write a generic or blanket cover letter, specifically targeting your cover letter to each position you apply for is a big part of what will land you the job. Without investing time and effort into your cover letters, you're probably not going to get the interview, regardless of your qualifications.

My first tip in writing an effective cover letter is to draw a connection between your qualifications and your education. This isn't always easy, but it is what will make you stand out in the mind of the employer.

Start by taking the job posting and listing the criteria the employer is looking for. Then list the skills and experience you have. Either address how your skills match the job in paragraph form or list the criteria and your qualifications in bulleted form.

Effective cover letters explain the reasons for your interest in the specific organization and identify your most relevant skills or experiences (remember, relevance is determined by the employer's self-interest). The letter should express a high level of interest, excitement and knowledge about the position.

To be effective, your cover letter should follow the basic format of a typical business letter and should address three general issues:

1. *First Paragraph*: Why you are writing.

2. *Middle Paragraphs*: What you have to offer.

3. *Concluding Paragraph*: How you will follow-up.

In some cases, a friend or acquaintance may have referred you to a potential employer. Be sure to mention this mutual contact, by name, up front in the cover letter since it is likely to encourage your reader to keep reading.

If you are writing in response to a job posting, indicate where you learned of the position and the title of the position. More importantly, express your enthusiasm and the likely match between your credentials and the position's qualifications.

If you are writing a prospecting letter to inquire about possible job openings, state your specific job objective. Since this type of letter is unsolicited, it is even more important to capture the reader's attention.

If you are writing a networking letter to approach an individual for information, make your request clear. The advantage to writing a letter like this and including your resume is that you will be making contacts in the business world and when a job opening comes up, they may still have your resume on file. It never hurts to be proactive when looking for a job!

In responding to an advertisement, refer specifically to the qualifications listed and illustrate how your particular abilities and experiences relate to the position for which you are applying. In a prospecting letter, express your potential to fulfill the employer's needs rather than focus on what the employer can offer you.

You can do this by giving evidence that you have researched the organization thoroughly and that you possess skills used within that organization.

Emphasize your achievements and problem-solving skills. Show how your education and work skills are transferable, and thus relevant, to the position for which you are applying.

Close by reiterating your interest in the job and letting the employer know how they can reach you, including your phone number and/or email address. If you want, you can make a bid directly for the job interview or informational interview and indicate that you will follow-up with a telephone call to set up an appointment at a mutually convenient time. Be sure to make the call within the time frame indicated.

In some instances, an employer may explicitly prohibit phone calls or you may be responding to a "blind want-ad," which precludes you from this follow-up. Unless this is the case, make your best effort to reach the organization. At the very least, you should confirm that your materials were received and that your application is complete.

If you are applying from outside the employer's geographic area you may want to indicate if you'll be in town during a certain time frame (this makes it easier for the employer to agree to meet with you).

Here are the key rules in making a good resume cover letter:

- No punctuation, grammar, spelling, and construction errors should be spotted on the letter.

- Write the correct address and the name of the proper person that should receive your letter.

- Avoid the phase: "To whom it may concern." This signals that you have not researched the company.

- Make your resume cover letter tailor-made to the particular company you are writing to.

- Never copy from other sources and keep it original.

- Make sure you know the company and the job you are targeting. The employer knows and feels how much the applicant wants the position through the resume cover letter.

- Use proper diction and terms.

In conclusion, you may indicate that your references are available upon request. Also, if you have a portfolio or writing samples to support your qualifications, state their availability.

Now, we've covered the three most important documents you need in a job search: the resume, the cover letter, and the reference sheet. The next chapter will provide you with a review of the most important points you need to insure are captured in your resume presentation.

Checklists for Success

I know you want to get moving so you can get the job you seek, and you might even be ready now with your resume, reference sheet, and cover letter. Before you get all excited, however, and put your information in the mail, you will want to go through a few check points to insure success.

First and foremost, run a spell check on your computer. Then, read through your documents twice to make sure there are no typographical or grammatical errors. It might also help to have someone else read over them as well to be sure you didn't miss anything. The more people that see your resume, the more likely it is that misspelled words and awkward phrases will be seen and corrected, making your resume that much more impressive to potential employers.

Cover Letter Checklist:

- The contact name and company name are correct.

- The letter is addressed to an individual, if possible.

- The cover letter mentions the position you are applying for and where it was listed.

- Your personal information is all included and correct.

- If you have a contact at the company, mention him or her in the first paragraph of your cover letter.

- The cover letter is targeted to the position you are applying for.

- The letter is focused, concise, clear, and well organized.

- If you have a gap in your employment history, explain it in your cover letter.

- The font is easy to read.

- No spelling or grammatical errors are present.

- Read the cover letter out loud to make sure there are no missing words.

- The cover letter is printed on good quality bond paper matching your resume.

- You have kept a copy for yourself.

- Your letter is signed.

When it comes to your resume, there are also a few things to keep in mind. Much is the same as for the cover letter, but you want your resume to be tip top as well.

Resume Checklist:

- There are no typographical or spelling errors.

- The format is consistent throughout the entire document.

- Use a good quality paper that is heavier than regular copy paper.

- You may want to use a colored paper, but make sure it is not garish like hot pink or neon green. Cream, gray, and off white are always good choices.

- Use 8 ½" x 11" paper.

- Print on only one side.

- Use a font between 10 and 14. You want it to be easy to read and look pleasant to the eye.

- Use non-decorative fonts, but don't be afraid to experiment and use something a little interesting – just not TOO interesting!

- Stick to one font.

- Avoid italics, scripts, and underlined words except for when underlining your headings.

- Do not use horizontal or vertical lines, graphics, or shading.

- Do not fold or staple your resume.

- If you must mail your resume, put it in a large envelope and mail flat.

- Be sure there is enough postage on the envelope to make it to the company.

- When at all possible, deliver your resume in person and ask to speak with the personnel director when you do so.

- Follow up after a reasonable period of time if you have not heard anything. This shows initiative on your behalf and makes you memorable in the mind of the person doing the hiring.

Well, we've done a lot of talking about how to craft a resume and cover letter that gets attention, but what if all this seems too tedious to you and you want to find an easier solution. That's what the next section is all about.

Resume Outsourcing & Resume Templates

As I mentioned earlier, your resume is an advertising tool and you are the product. If a product is advertised poorly, it will barely make it off the launching pad no matter how great the product is. You are marketing yourself with your resume and that's not something you want to leave up to chance, especially if what is at stake here is your future.

If you've made it this far in this book and you are feeling overwhelmed about writing your own resume, there are several options available to you.

Resume Writing Services

The first option is to hire a resume writing service. This is often the best option because these companies help you create professional resumes that will increase your chances of making it to the job interview. The investment you make in hiring a professional will far outweigh the time and energy you will spend writing your own and the possibility of a poor end result.

Since your aim is to provide your reader with an attractive and job-winning resume, the resume writer would make things easy for you by offering several different sample resumes as the basis for your own resume. All you have to do is to choose the most suited one for you.

The use of resume writers is applicable to any type of career. They offer resumes for military, office management, production management, teaching, restaurant, real estate, programmers, technical writing, legal jobs, journalism, human resources, counseling, marketing, accounting, college students, and many more. No matter what type of person you are, you are assured you will get the particular type of resume suited for the job you choose.

Resume writers are able to offer you a roster of great styles, fonts, text colors, backgrounds, and other themes that will surely generate enough attention and get noticed by any reader. In this way, your resume can have a great chance of putting you at the top of the pile.

Best of all, professional resume writers have been there and done that. They know how to make a resume everything it should be. They know when they can push the guidelines and when they can't. They know how to make you stand out without going overboard. Resume services are staffed with professionals who make your success their own.

Resume services have the experience to spot your strength, focus on your abilities and position you as the ideal person for the job.

Professional resume writers generally charge between $90 and $200, but that is a fair price considering the advantages it gives you. I suggest that you don't pick a resume service based on price alone. Different resume service companies and professionals can have different approaches and varying degrees of success. Be sure to do your research before hiring a professional and find out their success rates, their number of years in the industry, the complementary services they provide and any other considerations that could give you the assurance that you are investing in the right resume service.

It is wise to invest in your resume because in the long run, resume writing services can save you money. Remember, when you are unemployed, everyday that passes mean expenses that aren't being paid, not to mention the drain to savings if you are lucky enough to have some. Every time you send out a resume and you get no results, it is a drain on your resources. Plus, the added stress of waiting in anticipation for a response that may or may not come can take its toll over time.

Resume writing services are there to make sure that you get the best chance possible. They are in the business of producing well-organized resumes that position you to win the job.

Online Resume Templates

Another solution is to use online resume templates. Many of them are free and are quite easy to use. In using these templates, all you do is type over the existing text provided on the samples, and you end up with a good, professional and functional resume that can then be printed out.

There are also free resume builders that let you save those precious hours thinking about what to write or what to include on your resume. They offer an easy to use interface that only requires you to choose what style you want to use and then you answer questions to determine what will be included on your resume. By filling in the necessary fields, your resume is done before you know it.

Choices of fonts, text colors, backgrounds, lines and tables, and structures are all available.

The finished resume can be downloaded as a Word document or can be converted to an html file, perfect if you want to post it on the Internet or if you have your own website. With free resume builder, creating your resume is easy, fast, and free.

Here are some online resume templates to try:

http://resumecompanion.com/
http://www.livecareer.com/resume-builder
http://www.theresumebuilder.com/

http://www.gotresumebuilder.com/

http://resumizer.com/

http://www.emurse.com/

Choosing the Right Resume Format

There are three main acceptable resume formats available: the chronological format, the functional format and the combination format. All have different purposes and can be used differently for what is best suited for a particular requirement.

Chronological Format:

The chronological format is the most popular in the world of resumes. An example of the the major components that should be included in this format are:

1) Objective Statement

2) Work History and Experiences

3) Education and Achievements

4) Personal Data Section

5) Professional Affiliation Section

6) Reference Section

This resume style is best for emphasizing achievements and professional contributions in an easily readable order. It highlights successions in career growth and professional development.

What you do with this format is start with the latest achievement or employer and work backwards. Most employers who will call you to the interview will be interested in the latest company, the position you held and the contribution you made. This is why this format works best for the applicant who wants his career achievements emphasized and noticed at first glance.

Functional Format:

The functional resume format is often used by people who have changed jobs and careers and for those who have had gaps in their employment histories. An example of the important components of this format is:

1) Objective Statement

2) Summary of Qualifications / Profile

3) Relevant Skills and Experience / Accomplishments

4) Employment History

5) Education and Professional Development

6) The Professional Affiliation Section

The purpose of this resume is to emphasize your skills. Note that while technical proficiencies and skills are the main focus during the presentation, they do not necessarily have to be in order. The skills that you want presented upfront should be the skills you think the employer needs, so that the interview focuses largely on your core competencies.

Combination Format:

The combination format is a combination of focusing on your skills while also retaining a chronological presentation of work histories and relevancies. An example of the way this format lays out is:

1) Objective Statement

2) Profile

3) Accomplishments

4) Education and Achievements

By learning about these different resume formats, you will be able to compare the advantages and disadvantages of each and determine which will work best for you.

Online Resume Formats

If you would like to include your resume online, special formats should be used. These are HTML, PDF, and ASCII Text. Unlike the offline resume formats, online resumes need to include Internet codes.

Hyper Text Markup Language (HTML): This is a type of web language used in document layout for web browsers. The language controls all the formatting styles including: fonts, layouts, paragraphs, margins, colors, links, and tables. For those who are familiar with the language, it is very simple. But for those who are new to HTML, the codes can be extremely confusing and intimidating. For example, HTML codes begin with

<H1> and end with </H1>. Other codes include <HTML> <HEAD> that end with </HTML> </HEAD> and <p> ending with </p> and there are many more. If you are going to use HTML to create your online resume, be mindful of the codes. Any error on one of the codes will mean a different final display of the online resume.

Portable Document Format (PDF): This is a popular file format exclusively used by Adobe Acrobat. This type is being used more and more as a substitute for HTML. With a PDF, you can create online resumes that present the exact image you want your readers to see. In other words, what you create is exactly what your readers will see. There is no difference from computer to computer (a problem often encountered on files such as Word documents). However, if you create an online resume in PDF format, the recipient needs to have an Adobe Reader for them to be able to see. The good thing is that the Adobe Acrobat is readily available to be downloaded from the net and most people have it these days anyway.

American Standard Code for Information Interchange (ASCII): This online format is used as a formatting style by many who want to post their resume on an online job board. This format is also used when an online resume is sent through email. To avoid any errors while using ASCII, the document should remain left justified. The document should also avoid the use of bullets. Instead, a dash (-) or an asterisk (*) can be an alternative.

Any of these 3 formats would make a good online resume. It is up to you what type of format you prefer.

Resume Samples

There are literally hundreds of different ways you can write a resume and so many formats you can use, that it can be quite confusing. There are a lot of sites on the Internet that can provide you with free templates that just require you to insert your personal information and then print it out, but I have compiled some sample resumes for you in this chapter as well.

You can use these as an outline for your own as resume, but keep in mind that you are mostly using samples for the formatting, not the wording. Follow the information in this book to help you word your resume uniquely and effectively, and use the samples to help you choose a layout that you like.

Keep the type of job in mind when you are determining how to layout or design your resume.

For example, if you are applying for a creative job, it is okay to be creative with your resume (but not too creative). A professional position, however, necessitates a more professional-looking resume.

No matter what way you decide to go with your layout, be sure your resume is eye-catching and intriguing. As I mentioned earlier, the resume is your first introduction to your potential employer, so you will want to make the best first impression you can right out of the gate.

Following are several samples for you to consider when crafting a resume. Choose the format that works best for your personality and the job position you seek, and use these as a guide to get started.

CHLOE ZABATSKI

123 Alpha Street • Las Vegas, NV 12345 • (123) 555-1234 • chloez@getthatjob.com

OBJECTIVE: A position as a Personal Assistant/Office Manager, allowing me to use my organizational and communication skills.

HIGHLIGHTS OF QUALIFICATIONS
- 15+ years experience providing outstanding administrative and personal support to a senior executive.
- A motivated self-starter, able to quickly grasp issues and attend to details while maintaining a view of the big picture. Expert in juggling multiple projects and achieving on-time completion within budget.
- Creative, resourceful and flexible, able to adapt to changing priorities and maintain a positive attitude and strong work ethic.
- A clear and logical communicator, able to establish rapport with both clients and colleagues, and monitor individuals to achieve organizational objectives.

PROFESSIONAL EXPERIENCE
1988-present PERSONAL ASSISTANT & OFFICE MANAGER
Paige & Associates, Denver, CO
Personal Assistant
- Provided continuous, high quality support to President/CEO. Coordinated schedule, appointments and travel arrangements; managed expense account and recovery.
- Proofed and edited speeches, reports and press releases; screened calls and communicated directives to Board members and company shareholders.
- Managed President's securities portfolio and prepared regulatory filings as needed. Acted as liaison to stockbrokers, accountants and legal counsel.
- Organized annual shareholder meetings, including site selection, catering and preparation of appropriate materials.
- Planned two major relocations: Assisted in site selection, worked with architect on interior design, and oversaw equipment/furniture/telecommunications setup without interruption in operations.

Office Manager
- Coordinated workflow among five consultants and supervised three support staff. Prioritized and delegated tasks, provided motivation and direction to create a positive work environment and ensured accurate, on-time completion.
- Tracked office expenses and created monthly reports for senior executive. Prepared invoices, Accounts Receivable/Payable and banking.
- Mediated conflicts among employees and between staff and management, utilizing diplomacy and humor to resolve issues.
- Responded to client needs and provided additional support where necessary.

Additional experience includes:
Seminar and Retreat Coordinator, Mediation, Inc., Reno, NV
On-site Massage Therapist, Reno Corporate Massage, Reno, NV

EDUCATION & TRAINING
B.A., Psychology, American University, Washington, DC
CMT/Somatic Educator, Somatic Institute, New York, NY
Additional training includes: Stress Management and Meditation

109

RANDI B. JENKINS

134 Bluehill Cove • Port Washington, NY 12345 • 123-555-1234 • rbjenkins@getthatjob.com

OBJECTIVE: An opportunity obtain a marketing or marketing management position, with eventual advancement to vice president of marketing in a growth-oriented company.

HIGHLIGHTS OF QUALIFICATIONS

- May 2004 received MB.A. Degree with emphasis in Marketing
- Six years experience in program development, international marketing, and Internet marketing.
- Highly effective leading and motivating teams to produce positive results while meeting deadlines.
- Strong communication, interpersonal and presentation skills.

PROFESSIONAL MARKETING EXPERIENCE

COMTROTRON, New York, NY   2003 to 2004
Marketing Consultant/Graduate Student Intern
- Interned as marketing consultant for this international e-business development company.
- Became integral team member in the development of online marketing programs for clients including AT&T, Avon and Nike.
- Developed reports for clients including Avon's "Customer Needs and Reports Strategy."
- Conducted extensive research on the Internet, analyzed information, identified online solutions and reported results to project leaders and clients.

COOKING TIME INTERNATIONAL PUBLICATIONS, New York, NY   1998 to 2003
Publicity Manager
- Managed promotions and publicity campaigns for over 200 titles of international publishing company.
- Created promotional strategy, managed company website, and increased online promotions.
- Organized and conducted trade show presentations, promotional events and seminars.
- On several occasions, made guest appearances as a food expert for local network TV and radio stations.
- Made presentations on new directions and products at national and international cooking conferences.
- Supervised and trained staff of four including a publicist and marketing assistant.
- Pitched stories and secured placement in top 100 daily newspapers and high-profile magazines.
- Coordinated distribution of collateral such as catalogs, brochures and point-of-sale materials.

LONDONMIST FRAGRANCES, London, England   1997-1998
Assistant to Publicity Director/Student Intern
- Assisted in coordination of promotional campaign that launched EveningMist line product, "Shades."
- Maintained departmental records and correspondence, coordinated and scheduled meetings.

EDUCATION & TRAINING

M.B.A., Marketing, New York University, New York, NY   2004

Relevant Coursework	Brand Management	Marketing Strategy	Sales Channel Mgt.
Data Analysis	Sports & Events Mktg.	Global Management	Strategic Advantage
Leadership	Decision Modeling	Managerial Finance	Managerial Accounting

B.A., History, Adelphi College, Garden City, NY   1997

Technical Skills – Illustrator, Photoshop, Filemaker, MS Access, Excel, PowerPoint, QuarkXpress

SARA FREMONT

123 Oak Lane ~ St. Louis, Missouri 12345

314-555-1212   saraf@getthatjob.com

EDUCATOR
DRIVER & TRAFFIC SAFETY

Patient and caring Professional committed to helping students learn. Certified in driver and traffic safety from Midwest State University. Memberships include ADTSEA (American Driver Traffic Safety Education Association), MDTSEA (Midwest Driver Traffic Safety Education Association), and the National Association of Female Executives. Additional background as a Missouri Licensed Property Casualty Insurance Agent for Home, Auto, Health and Life.

CERTIFICATION, LICENSURE & EDUCATION

MIDWEST STATE UNIVERSITY, St. Louis, Missouri
Driver/Traffic Safety Education Certification, August 2002

~ Renewal of Missouri Educators License K-8, July 2002

MISSOURI EDUCATORS COLLEGE, St. Louis, Missouri
Graduate Level Coursework in Education, 1989-1990
GPA: 3.83/4.00

Bachelor of Science Degree in Elementary Education, 1976
Semester Honors: 3.47/4.00   Semester Highest Honors: 4.00/4.00
Awarded compensated internship (for teaching)

PROFESSIONAL EXPERIENCE

FIRST CHOICE INSURANCE COMPANY, St. Louis, Missouri   April 1990 – July 2000
Insurance Agent
- Managed insurance agency daily operations, including territories and accounts.
- Fielded and resolved insurance sales questions, generated leads.
- Developed customer quotations and completed applications.
- Hired, trained and motivated support personnel.
- Assessed client needs and established long-term client relationships.

Achievements:
- Acknowledged as line leader of a four state territory for loss ratio, retention and customer service.
- Exceeded measured performance standards per ratio each of 10 years.

S&D RAILROAD COMPANY, St. Louis, Missouri   March 1979 – November 1987
Conductor
- Responsible for movement of freight traffic between pre-determined destinations.

Achievements
- The first female to be employed by this train service.
- Promoted from entry-level position within a very short period of time.

FRONTENAC SCHOOL DISTRICT, Frontenac, Missouri   October 1972 – March 1979
Transportation Department, Building & Grounds, and Substitute Teacher
- Employed during entire collegiate experience 20-40 hours per week.

111

Jane Doe

123-555-1234 ~ dtoor@getthatjob.com

40 Village Drive ~ Charlotte, NC 12345

Artist

Award-winning designer with degrees in Textiles and Oriental Painting. Background includes exhibiting work at the Manchester Gallery and successfully completing an internship with Ralston Technology in the United States. Fluent in English, Spanish and Russian.

Awards & Exhibitions

- Third Place, LG Chemicals Design Contest, sponsored by LG Chemicals, Ltd., 1996
- Second Place, Textile Design Contest, sponsored by US Federation of Textile Industries, 1995
- Third Place, Noonan Design Contest, sponsored by the Noonan Company, 1995
- Third Place, US Modern Art Concours, 1994
- Four-time Recipient, Department Scholarship, 1992-1994

    o Department of Textiles Art Degree Exhibition, 1997
    o Best Graduate Exhibition, Manchester Gallery, 1995
    o Department of Oriental Painting Degree Exhibition, 1995
    o US Modern Art Exhibition, 1994

Professional Experience

PALSTON TECHNOLOGY, INC., New York, NY   1999 to 2000
Intern, Art Department
- Successfully completed the presentation CD involving draping cars for Hyundai Motor Company of Korea.
- Concluded training for the Artworks Studio software GTxL cutter system.
- Traveled to Atlanta for the Bobbin Americas Expo from September 30 to October 2, 1999

FIRST IMPORTS CHANNEL CO., LTD, London, UK   1997-1998
Designer, Flooring Design Department
- Designed flooring products and conducted market research to determine client needs.
- Ensured quality of color matching by working closely with the manufacturer.

Education

WESTFALL UNIVERSITY, Bridgeport, Connecticut
Bachelor of Fine Arts, Department of Textile Art, 1997

NEW HAVEN COLLEGE, New Haven, Connecticut
Bachelor of Fine Arts, Department of Oriental Painting, 1995

SARA LIVINGSTON

1213 Flower Street ~ Beverly Hills, California 12345
123-555-1234 ~ sara@getthatjob.com

OVERVIEW OF QUALIFICATIONS

- Award-winning multi-lingual Interior Designer with an outstanding background in set design for NBC's *The Templetons*, Tri-Star's *Edge of Paradise*, and *Carrolton Returns* on PBS.
- High profile clientele includes Burt Williams, Trevor Sanders, Liz MacQuire and R. Fredericks.
- Fluent in English, Spanish, Portuguese, German and Italian; certified by the Design Institute of New York and Los Angeles; licensed designer in the United Kingdom, France and Italy.

OUTSTANDING PROFESSIONAL ACCOMPLISHMENTS

- Chosen as *Designer of the Decade* in 1999 for work on *The Templetons* series.
- Received special Academy Award in 1992 for work on *Edge of Paradise*.
- Featured in *Vanity Fair, Time Magazine, Newsweek, Elle* and *Interior Design*.
- Recognized as the youngest design entrepreneur with the Launching of *Designs by Sara*.

EMPLOYMENT HISTORY

DESIGNS BY SARA, New York, Los Angeles, Rome and London   1990 - 2001
Founder / President
- Established interior design/boutique catering to high net-worth clientele, including stars of stage, screen and television.
- Oversaw daily operations, including purchasing, outsourcing and client relations.
- Collaborated with online firm for *Designs by Sara* training course accredited by the Design Institute of New York and Los Angeles.
- Grew company from $.5 million in 1990 to $6 million annually in 1993.
- Recruited, trained and directed activities of 17 design professionals.
- Launched satellite offices in Los Angeles in 1992, Rome in 1993 and London in 1994.
- Wrote weekly column in the *Los Angeles Times Magazine* on affordable interior design.
- Appeared on local newscasts with design tips.

COVENTRY INTERIORS, New York, NY   1989 – 1990
Intern
- Participated in client/designer meetings.
- Created design for firm's reception area that was chosen as best among 20 interns.
- Assisted junior designers with fabric, furniture and accessory selection.

ACADEMIC BACKGROUND

DESIGN INSTITUTE OF NEW YORK, New York, Los Angeles, Rome and London
- *Master of Arts in Interior Design*, 1989
- Awarded the Francois Designation for Outstanding Interior Design Work, 1988-1989

DESIGN INSTITUTE OF LOS ANGELES, Los Angeles, CA
- *Bachelor of Arts in Interior Design*, 1988

ASSOCIATIONS

- *Vice-President*, **Interior Designers of America, 1999-Present**
- *Member*, **European Designers, 1997-Present**

Tom Fitzgerald

100 Overtown Road
Portland, Oregon 12345
123-555-1234 ~ tom@getthatjob.com

PROFILE

- Seasoned Professional with 20 years of experience in sales and sales management.
- Consistently awarded for outstanding performance; repeatedly won the *President's Club Award*, placing in the top 10% of company sales nationwide.
- Excels in public relations, marketing, human resources and procedures administration.
- Licensed Real Estate Agent in the states of Oregon and California.
- Facilitates financial and business decisions for resort real estate companies.

EXPERIENCE

SALES MANAGEMENT
- Recruited, interviewed, hired and trained all sales personnel.
- Managed all public relations, marketing and sales for *Seasons Plus Resorts*, the largest vacation ownership company in the world.
- Developed an elite, goal-centered, cooperative sales force.
- Implemented and monitored productive property owner referral program.
- Directed site that was judged #1 within company in revenue per guest.

SALES
- Sold resort home sites as well as vacation properties to a marketed clientele.
- Won numerous awards as top performer and closer at all levels, including *President's Club Award* for sales in top 10% of the company nationwide.
- Directed building and sales of speculative property.
- Successfully completed sales leadership courses: "Date to Soar" and "7 Habits of Highly Successful People."

ADMINISTRATION
- Grew company to $.5 million annual sales, broadened business scope from constructing small home to developing high-end real estate properties.
- Bought property and oversaw home construction from start to finish.
- Hired all subcontractors and managed all payroll, insurance and taxes.

EMPLOYMENT

Director of Sales/Sales Manager, Seasons Resorts, Portland, OR	2/99 – Present
Owner, Tom Fitzgerald Construction, Redding, CA	6/90 – 12-98
Sales Professional, Seasons Resorts, Portland, OR	6/85 – 5/90
Sales Professional, World Resorts, Portland, OR	4/82 – 5/85

EDUCATION

CIVIL ENGINEERING **Western Tech**, Portland, OR	9/76 – 5/78
BUSINESS **California Community College**, Redding, CA	9/75 – 5/76

Cover Letter Samples

As you have learned, the cover letter can be just as important as the resume, so you will want it to look as professional and intriguing as possible. In the following pages, I have included a few sample letters that you may want to use as templates for crafting your own cover letters.

7 Apple Court
Eugene, OR 97401
503-555-0303

Mr. Archie Weatherby
California Investments, Inc.
25 Sacramento Street
San Francisco, CA 94102

Dear Mr. Weatherby,

My outgoing personality, my sales experience, and my recently completed education make me a strong candidate for a position as an insurance broker for California Investments, Inc.

I recently graduated from the University of Oregon with a degree in marketing, where I was president of both the Future Business Leaders of America and the American Marketing Association.

Although a recent graduate, I am not a typical new graduate. I attended school in Michigan, Arizona, and Oregon. And I've put myself through these schools by working such jobs as radio advertising sales, newspaper subscription sales, and bartending, all of which enhanced my formal education.

I have the maturity, skills, and abilities to embark on a career in insurance brokering, and I'd like to do this in California, my home state.

I will be in California at the end of this month, and I'd like very much to talk with you concerning a position at California Investments. I will follow up this letter with a phone call to see if I can arrange a time to meet with you.

Thank you for your time and consideration.

Sincerely,

John Oakley

23 Hickory Tree Way
Belle Mead, NJ 08502
(908) 555-7495

September 12, 2006

Ms. Kristin Heller
The Research Institute
34 Marketing Court
Princeton, NJ 08540

Dear Ms. Heller,

As marketing companies are increasingly called upon to supply information on magazine readership to publishers, there is a growing need for trained and experienced professionals in the field.

Through my marketing/research experiences and my master's thesis, which have particularly dealt with improving marketing research studies so they can better define magazine audiences to potential advertisers, I am certain I could give you valuable assistance in satisfying research demands, managing key projects, and improving the marketing tools you currently use.

I will be completing my master's degree in December and would be interested in making a significant contribution to the Research Institute's profitability in a marketing/research capacity.

I am sure my services would be useful to you, and I will call you in early October to discuss an interview.

Thank you for your time and consideration.

Sincerely,

Scott Morris

1090 Peachtree Lane, #4
Atlanta, GA 30303
404/555-3030

Ms. Judy Sumner
Atlanta Board of Education
45 Peachtree Blvd.
Atlanta, GA 30303

Dear Ms. Sumner,

Perhaps I am the "multi-talented teacher" you seek in your "Multi-Talented Teacher" advertisement in today's Atlanta Constitution. I'm a versatile teacher, ready to substitute, if necessary, as early as next week. I have the solid teaching experience you specify as well as the strong computer skills you desire.

I am presently affiliated with a highly regarded private elementary school. Mr. Craig, the headmaster, will certainly give you a good reference. The details of your advertisement suggest to me that the position will involve many of the same responsibilities that I am currently performing.

In addition to the planning, administration, and student-parent counseling duties I highlight in my resume, please note that I have a master's degree as well as a teaching certificate from the state of Georgia.

Knowing how frantic you must be without a fifth grade teacher, I will call you in a few days. Or if you agree upon reviewing my letter and resume that I am the teacher you need, call me at the home number listed above, or at 555-7327 during business hours.

Thanking you most sincerely for your time and consideration.

Cordially,

Maria Plazza-Smith

The previous samples give you a good idea of how others have created their cover letters, but I also wanted to provide you with some templates to work from. You'll find them on the next few pages.

Your Name
Your Address
Your City, State, Zip Code
Your Phone Number
Your Email

Date

Name
Title
Organization
Address
City, State, Zip Code

Dear Mr./Ms. Last Name:

First Paragraph: Why You Are Writing. Remember to include the name of a mutual contact, if you have one. Be clear and concise regarding your request.

Middle Paragraphs: What You Have to Offer. Convince the readers that they should grant the interview or appointment you requested in the first paragraph. Make connections between your abilities and their needs or your need for information and their ability to provide it. Remember, you are interpreting your resume. Try to support each statement you make with a piece of evidence. Use several shorter paragraphs rather than one large block of text.

Final Paragraph: How You Will Follow Up. Remember, it is your responsibility to follow-up; this relates to your job search. State that you will do so and provide the professional courtesy of indicating when (one week's time is typical). You may want to reduce the time between sending out your resume and follow up if you fax or e-mail it.

Sincerely,

Your Signature

Your Typed Name

Your Name
Your Address
Your City, State, Zip Code
Your Phone Number
Your Email

Date

Name
Title
Organization
Address
City, State, Zip Code

Dear Mr./Ms. Last Name:

Your Requirements:

- Responsible for evening operations in Student Center and other facilities, including managing registration, solving customer problems, dealing with risk management and emergencies, enforcement of department policies.
- Assists with hiring, training, and management of staff.
- Experience in the supervision of student staff and strong interpersonal skills are also preferred.
- Experience in collegiate programming and management.

My Qualifications:

- Register students for courses, design and manage program software, solve customer problems, enforce department policies, and serve as a contact for students, faculty, and staff.
- Hiring, training, scheduling and management of staff, managing supply inventory, and ordering.
- Extensive experience in collegiate programming and management.
- Excellent interpersonal and communication skills.

I appreciate your taking the time to review my credentials and experience. Again, thank you for your consideration.
Sincerely,

Your Signature

Your Typed Name

Your name
Mailing address
City, state, and zip
Telephone number(s)
Email address
Today's date

Your addressee's name
Professional title
Organization name
Mailing address
City, state and zip

Dear Mr. (or Ms.) last name,

Start your letter with a grabber—a statement that establishes a connection with your reader, a probing question, or a quotable quote. Briefly say what job you are applying for.

The mid-section of your letter should be one or two short paragraphs that make relevant points about your qualifications. You should not summarize your resume! You may incorporate a column or bullet point format here.

Your last paragraph should initiate action by explaining what you will do next (e.g., call the employer) or instigate the reader to contact you to set up an interview. Close by saying "thank you."

Sincerely yours,

Your handwritten signature
Your name (typed)

Your Name
Your Address
Your City, State, Zip Code
Your Phone Number
Your Email Address

Date

Employer Name
Title
Company
Address
City, State, Zip Code
Salutation

Dear Mr./Ms.

The body of your cover letter lets the employer know what position you are applying for, why the employer should select you for an interview, and how you will follow-up.

The first paragraph of your letter should include information on why you are writing. Mention the position you are applying for. Include the name of a mutual contact, if you have one. Be clear and concise regarding your request.

The next section of your cover letter should describe what you have to offer the employer. Convince the reader that they should grant the interview or appointment you requested in the first paragraph. Make strong connections between your abilities and their needs. Mention specifically how your skills and experience match the job you are applying for. Remember, you are interpreting your resume, not repeating it. Try to support each statement you make with a piece of evidence. Use several shorter paragraphs or bullets rather than one large block of text.

Conclude your cover letter by thanking the employer for considering you for the position. Include information on how you will follow-up. State that you will do so and indicate when (one week's time is typical). You may want to reduce the time between sending out your resume and follow up if you fax or e-mail it.

Respectfully yours,

Handwritten Signature (for a mailed letter)
Typed Signature

Reference Sheet Samples

While your Reference Sheet will not be mailed along with your resume and cover letter, you will still need to have it on hand during an interview so that you can produce it immediately when your potential employer asks for it.

In this chapter, I have provided some sample reference sheets for you to use when creating your own.

CARRIE E. COMPLETE

PRESENT ADDRESS
123 Hawkins Graduate House
West Lafayette, IN 47906
(317) 555-1123

PERMANENT ADDRESS
12334 N. College Avenue
Indianapolis, IN 46220
(317) 555-1829

REFERENCES

Professor John English
Sociology Department
Purdue University
Stone Hall
West Lafayette, IN 47907
(317) 555-6000

Professor English is my academic advisor and is presently supervising my research in an independent study sociology course.

Mrs. Diana Handie
Food Services Supervisor
Hawkins Graduate House
Purdue University
West Lafayette, IN 47907
(317) 555-2323

Mrs. Handie was my supervisor when I worked in the
Hawkins Cafeteria.

Mrs. Jennifer Active
Activity Therapy Staff Wabash Valley Mental Health Center
2900 North River Road
West Lafayette, IN 47906
(317) 564-9600

Mrs. Active is my current employer.

References for James Esterman

433 Colby Hall
Hutchinson University
Hutchinson, IL 60353
(847-555-2733)
esterjo1@hutch.edu

Dr. Par Wombat
Professor of Psychology
Hutchinson University
Hutchinson, IL 60353
847-555-3212

Dr. Wombat was my
visor in the Human
Subjects Research Lab

Dr. Chris Murphy
Professor of Biology
Hutchinson University
Hutchinson, IL 60353
847-555-3212

Dr. Murphy was my super-
professor in Biology 425

Mr. Michael McCollins
Project Manager
The Acme Corporation
112221 Main Street
Hutchinson, IL 60353
847-555-2813

Mr. McCollins supervised
my internship at the Acme
Corporation

Ms. Sonia Ramirez
Manager
The Rasmussen Corp.
312-555-2733
Chicago, IL 60105
312-555-2733

Ms. Ramirez supervised
my co-op experience at
the Rasmussen Corp.

IM A SAMPLE
1234 North 55 Street
Bellevue, Nebraska 68005
(402) 292-2345
iasample@aol.com

PROFESSIONAL REFERENCES

Name
Position
Title
Company
Address City, State, Zip Code
Company Phone Number

(Examples)
Bernard E. Langer
Director, Human Resources
Attaboy Company
7833 Avenue G
Omaha, NE 68134
(402) 738-4467

Dr. Sandra P. Doolittle
Chemistry Professor
Bellevue University
1000 Galvin Road South
Bellevue, NE 68005
(402) 293-5543

Gregory J. Throckmortan (Former Supervisor)
General Manager
Iowa Western Beef Company
234 6th Avenue
Council Bluffs, IA 51510
(712) 355-7865

At this point, you may have your resume out there and you may even have received some calls for interviews. In the next section, I will go over some interviewing tips so you can be prepared when you are face to face with a prospective employer as well.

Interviewing 101

The first thing you want to remember about being at a job interview is that first impressions count in a huge way.

Dress appropriately for the job. Never wear jeans to a job interview. It doesn't matter how casual the job is that you are applying for, jeans are inappropriate in any situation.

For women, a nice skirt and shirt or a suit is what is expected. For men, a suit is almost always expected, but you can get away with a pair of khaki pants and a nice polo shirt on some occasions.

When you are talking to your interviewer, be enthusiastic about the job. Convey your excitement about the possibility of working for the company and be sure to smile.

If you are applying for a creative position, you should bring along a portfolio of your work so that you can show off your creativity. This will usually be expected of you. Be sure that your portfolio is professionally put together, and is not sloppy in any way.

Your job interview is where you get the chance to shine. Be sure to answer all of the questions accurately and with enthusiasm. Try not to hesitate, and be prepared for anything to come up. I have heard cases when an employer asked the person applying for a sales position to sell him a pen. You will want to be ready to think on your feet when you are asked to do unexpected things like that.

Being prepared for your interview is the most important thing you can do. While you can't be prepared for everything that might come up, you can certainly prepare yourself by thinking of questions that might come up and how you would answer them.

Always remember, your personality will play an important part in getting you the job, in addition to your experience and your education. Above everything else, be yourself, and be excited and enthusiastic about your possible job.

When you are happy about being there, it will show in your demeanor and your responses. I can't stress enough how much this can make a difference in getting the job and not getting the job. People often overlook other flaws in return for a great attitude, so make that your number one priority.

Conclusion

When you are looking for a job, having the right tools at your disposal is extremely important. Those tools include having a killer resume coupled with a compelling cover letter. If you put more effort into these components then your competition does, you set yourself up from the start to be well received by prospective employers. You will be giving yourself an edge.

Make sure you are the one that stands out over the competition so that you'll be the one that gets the interview and wins the hearts of the employer!

Take your time making your resume and be sure that it reflects who you are and what you can do. Let your resume speak for you and your abilities and be sure to follow up with all the companies you have submitted your resume to.

Good luck and happy job searching!

About the Author

Faith M. Davis is both an author and a freelance writer focusing on the subjects and industries she knows and loves most: marketing, freelance writing, copywriting, holistic health, wellness, self-help, metaphysics and inspirational topics.

Her articles have been featured globally in *Vitamin Publications, Wisdom Magazine, inspiremetoday.com* and *successtelevision.com.* As a freelance writer, she has written web copy, blogs, articles, brochure copy, advertisements, company profiles, press releases, email newsletters, landing pages, auto-responder emails, eBooks, special reports, marketing campaigns and more for various businesses in the holistic industry, and she has ghostwritten several books for best-selling authors.

As an author and copywriter with a background as a certified life coach, and as a lifetime participator in holistic health practices, she is uniquely qualified to write for the holistic industry. Her 10-year position as Director of Marketing at a thriving printing company in Pennsylvania has given her tremendous experience in marketing and copywriting, and when coupled with her love for everything holistic, her passion shines through.

Grab your free report by visiting her website: *"Marketing Mistakes That Can Destroy Your Holistic Business – 13 Solutions!"* www.faithmdavis.com

Connect with Faith Online:

www.facebook.com/WritingForHolisticLife
www.linkedin.com/in/faithmdavis
www.twitter.com/FaithMDavis

Made in the USA
Las Vegas, NV
15 February 2022

43962559R00079